THE *COMMUNITY* OF THE *ARK*

Mark Shepard

Simple Productions
12 East 15th Street, #3
Arcata, California 95521
USA

1990

hepard

பாnaraி ா ıuday

ISBN 0–938497–03–0 (trade paper)
LC Card #89–091948
Subject headings: Collective settlements—France;
Religious communities—France; Nonviolence

Printed on acid-free paper.
Manufactured in the United States of America.

10 9 8 7 6 5 4 3 2 1

Please write us for information on our other publications.

Acknowledgments

My thanks to the people of the Ark for their hospitality, and
especially to Jane Prentiss and Yvette Naal. Above all,
thanks to my mother, Lillian, whose financial and moral
support made this book possible.

We are accused of going against the times. We are doing that deliberately and with all our strength.

The machine enslaves, the hand sets free.

Lanza del Vasto

Tucked away in the windswept mountains of southern France is an island of peace known as the Community of the Ark.

This remarkable community—now in its fifth decade and numbering well over one hundred residents—is one of this century's most successful experiments in utopian living. Founded by Lanza del Vasto, a Christian disciple of Mahatma Gandhi, it offers an inspiring model for a nonviolent society.

I visited the Ark in 1979, sharing the life of the community for six weeks. This is the record of what I found.

La Borie Noble

The two-car electric train wound around the slopes of tree-covered mountains, and paused only briefly at the tiny station of Les Cabrils, a village of several houses. The station had already closed, and no one was there to meet me. The sun was on its way down; and, though this was mid-March in what I had imagined was sunny southern France, the weather was icy cold.

Then I noticed a sign: "La Communauté de l'Arche," pointing down the road. I started off quickly.

The road led along one slope of a steep, narrow valley. In about ten minutes, a building came into view, farther ahead on the opposite slope. Three stories, L-shaped, with a tower where the building's two wings met. Was that the Ark? Drawing nearer, I saw more buildings behind the first. Then a long strip of garden in the valley below the buildings.

The road took me down into the valley and up the other slope, to the foot of a stone staircase rising to the buildings above. As I reached the top steps, two women in long skirts were rushing by. I called out to them in my best brushed-up high school French, asking them to bring me to Nicole, the woman I had been told to contact. Pausing only long enough to puzzle out my French, they hurried me off with them to the big building I had seen first from the road.

Up some stone steps on the outside, through a kitchen, down a hall, through a massive wooden door, and—

pandemonium! Seventy people of all ages, milling around, talking, laughing. Women wearing blouses, sweaters, ankle-length skirts. Men in trousers, woolen sweaters, and vests. Strung from the necks of many, a wooden medallion: a cross with a quarter circle on each point, facing outward. Children raced among the legs of the adults.

I had lost the women who had ushered me here, so I began again asking for Nicole. One woman informed me I must see Jane, the woman from America, and went off to find her.

The room that housed this commotion was itself large, simple, elegant: long and low, with walls of stone covered by whitewashed plaster, and a floor of varnished pine. Candles in holders along the walls provided the lighting. In one corner, a large stone fireplace and a wood stove; in the other, a 6-foot-high panel sculpture of Noah. Overseeing the scene from high on an end wall: a framed drawing of Mahatma Gandhi.

In a few minutes, a cherubic face under a ridiculous floppy hat popped up before me.

"Hello, I'm Jane."

She explained that I had arrived at the tail end of the Festival of St. Joseph, which had been going on all day.

Now safely attached to Jane, I sat on the floor with the others, who were settling down to watch a comical skit: Snow White and the Seven Dwarves, performed by costumed adults and children. Following that, reed mats were unrolled along the edges of the room, and we settled down on them to a holiday dinner. A main course of *galettes de sarrasin*—buckwheat crêpes, folded over melted cheese—was accompanied by bread, salad, and wine. Afterwards, the floor was cleared for folk dancing. Young adults commanded the floor, as French and Israeli music poured from a battery-run phonograph.

But, after my hectic journey, I found myself falling asleep watching the dancers. Jane led me out by flashlight to a men's dormitory, where I went to bed with five woolen blankets.

Lanza del Vasto (Shantidas)

Where had they come from, these unorthodox and attractive people? And what had brought them to this obscure corner of France?

The answers reached back over four decades, to a young man named Joseph Jean Lanza del Vasto—son of an Italian noble family, artist, philosopher, poet, vagabond. At that time, Lanza was deeply troubled by what he saw as violence underlying the structures of European society—violence that had broken out as World War I, and that threatened to break out again. So in 1936 Lanza set out by boat to India, to meet the one person he thought might know how violence could be uprooted: Mahatma Gandhi.

Lanza spent three months with Gandhi in his ashram, absorbing the master's wisdom while learning to handspin cotton yarn. From Gandhi he heard not only of the means to confront injustice, but also of the evils of a culture based on centralized economy and government—a system that was ravaging the globe. And, in Gandhi's teachings, as well as in the ashram life itself, Lanza found keys to a way of life that might banish violence from society.

Gandhi, much taken with the imposing, aristocratic young man, gave him a new name: Shantidas, "Servant of Peace." The new convert returned to Europe in 1938 with the dream of starting a "Gandhian Order in the West."

But Lanza could find no recruits for his new Order—so he had to lay the idea aside. Over the ensuing years, his ideas about the Order gradually changed. Then, in Paris toward the end of World War II, Lanza began to attract a small following that would come to hear his talks on Gandhian philosophy and radical Christian lifestyle.

When the news of Gandhi's death came in 1948, Lanza felt the right time had come. He founded the first Community of the Ark on a small rented farm at Tournier, in the southwest of France. With him were five adults and four children; others soon arrived. The object was to create a community of people living by the Gandhian/Christian ideals of strict nonviolence and simplicity, while also cultivating the inward spiritual state from which practice of those ideals naturally emerged. By this community, Lanza hoped to show to others how a society based on these ideals would look, as well as to prove such a society feasible.

The Ark had another purpose as well. As the name implied, the community would hopefully be a haven from what Lanza saw as the coming self-destruction of Western society—a destruction fueled by greed, ignorance, violence, and a technology that magnified all these. He believed that those who stood apart from society might survive, and could then help build a new society on a saner foundation.

Despite these noble ideas and intentions, this first community at Tournier was a fiasco. Many who came couldn't live up to the demands of the community; many didn't understand or agree with the Ark's principles; some were mentally disturbed. All were accepted into the community, in the faith that nonviolence would convert all— but this proved overly ambitious. At the end of four years, Lanza quit the community in a fit of rage, declaring he would go to America to organize the Negroes.

But, soon after, Lanza and some others started up the community again on an estate near Bollène in the Rhone Valley. From this time on, anyone wanting to become a full member—a "Companion"—had to undergo a three-year novitiate, and then be approved unanimously by the other Companions.

Even so, the community grew, and after a decade was forced to look for a larger home. In 1963, the community bought a 1000-acre abandoned farm in the mountains of Languedoc in southern France, halfway between the towns of Béziers and Millau. Included on the land were several clusters of half-ruined buildings, made of stone in the traditional architecture of the region. As their new home, the Companions refurbished and added to one of these clusters, to form the "village" of La Borie Noble—where I was now staying.

Now, a decade and a half later, they had spread to two more "villages" on the land: Nogaret and La Flayssière. Altogether, the community now held about 125 residents, including Companions, novices, applicants, long-term visitors, and children. The residents came from almost every country of western Europe, and even farther. Though the Ark in its early days had drawn mostly intellectuals and aristocrats, residents now came from a wide range of backgrounds.

Besides this "mother community," the Ark had small beginnings of communities in other parts of France, as well as in Italy, Spain, and even Quebec. In all the communities combined, there were now about seventy Companions.

The Common Room

When I finally rose the next morning, I went looking for Jane, who was to be my official "hostess." She, like me, I had learned, was from San Francisco, where she had been involved with the Catholic Worker movement and its houses of hospitality for the poor. She would soon enter the final year of her novitiate here, and planned to return to the United States sometime to help found an American branch of the Ark.

I found her in the community kitchen I had quickly passed through the evening before. She and fifteen or twenty other women in blouses and long skirts were busy preparing both the day's lunch and supper, throwing cut-up food into huge pots on a large coal-burning stove. The stove threw off a heat I found welcome after the wintry chill of the other rooms I had been in.

I had missed the normal breakfast time, but Jane pulled out some wholewheat sourdough bread, butter, jam, and milk, all produced there in the community, and set me down at a large oak table in the next room. She no longer wore her ridiculous hat, and I would soon realize she was a good deal more mature than it had made her seem.

After breakfast, Jane sent me out to the barn to cut firewood with a visiting Spaniard named Francisco. With two-handled saws, we cut to size the wood stored there from the community's forests.

The work was interrupted on each hour by the pealing

of the bell in the tower of the main building, calling us sometimes to a moment of silent inward reflection, sometimes to a few minutes of prayer shared with others working nearby.

Despite these breaks, I found it rough going. Francisco kept telling me, "Ease up, let the saw do the work." I would quickly tire, and would rest while he split the thicker pieces with an axe.

By the end of the morning, I was exhausted. I said to Francisco, "I will have to become stronger."

Searching for the English, Francisco said, "It is not strength. You must find the right rhythm. Then the work will not be so hard."

At lunchtime, most of La Borie Noble's residents gathered in the Common Room, where the party had been held the evening before. Each took a bowl and spoon from a basket near the door, before sitting down on the reed mats rolled out along the edges of the room. There was much talk and laughter; children ran to sit with their favorite adults.

Big pots and trays were hauled in from the kitchen, and set on a low wooden table in the center of the room. In a short while, a male elder clapped his hands, and one of the women, Hirondelle, led the singing of the Ark's grace.

Lord, bless this meal
From which we draw the strength to serve you.
Give bread to those who haven't any,
And hunger and thirst for righteousness to those who
 have more than enough.

16

After this, one of the youngest children was sent with a basket of bread to the elder, who raised his hands over it and said a brief prayer. We then got up to fill our bowls at the table in the center of the room. The meal was vegetarian—the Companions refrain from killing animals—simple, yet with rich flavor: a whole grain, two cooked vegetables moistened with butter, salad, cheese, sourdough bread.

After most people had finished their meal, the elder clapped his hands again, and Hirondelle led a song of thanksgiving. As people became ready, each took their bowl and spoon to the kitchen to wash.

Afternoon work began about half an hour later. But, before sending me out again, Jane gave me a tour of La Borie Noble.

The village included about eight buildings of various sizes, all made from stone—some restored, some expanded, and some built from scratch. There were apartments for couples and families; a women's dormitory; a couple of barns; a cow shelter; a dairy; a stable for the horses used by the Ark's farmers. A carpentry shop held an assortment of hand tools hung on the walls—no machine tools. A large workbench in the center of the room was equipped with wooden leg vises tightened by wedges.

Another building housed both a small craft store and a school. In the school, the community's children were taught in a loose cross between Montessori methods and Gandhi's "basic education," an approach using practical hand labor as a lead-in to academic subjects.

For high school, I learned, the children either stayed in

the community or attended school in a nearby town, returning to the Ark on weekends. When they became adults, they were sent away from the community for at least three years, to see the "outside world." At the end of that time, they could choose whether to return to the Ark.

The store contained books, records, and handcrafts, for sale to visitors. Though no money was used within the community, the Ark still needed money to buy from the outside what it couldn't manage to produce. Most of that money came from this store, especially during the summer, when many visitors passed through; other money came from workshops and training camps put on by the Ark. All the money was held in common by the Companions, as was all other property, other than small personal items. Funds requests for personal expenditure, such as for medical treatment and occasional trips, were approved individually by the community.

We walked past a laundering facility, where clothes were washed by hand and brush in stone vats, with water piped in from a spring, a mile or so away. For the initial washing, the water was heated in an iron cauldron, by wood fire.

We again approached the main building, half of which had itself been built by the Companions. The upper floors were mostly taken up by residences.

Through a door on the building's ground level was a small room that was the Ark's bakery. (Maurice, the Italian baker, was gone at that time of day.) Shelves were lined with 12-pound round loaves of the wholewheat sourdough bread I had enjoyed at every meal there so far.

This bread was made by traditional methods, Jane told

me. It contained nothing but flour, salt, water, and starter; and the starter itself was made by setting out only flour mixed with water, letting it collect yeast naturally present in the air. Despite—or because of—its simplicity, it was the most delicious bread I had ever tasted.

Against one wall was a huge mixing bin, and at the end of the room was a wood-fired brick oven with a cast-iron door. Across the top of the oven door's frame, formed from the metal itself, were the words *"Je suis le pain de vie"* — "I am the bread of life."

As if to challenge the rest of the equipment, a large electric flour mill stood in the center of the room. Jane told me that electric lines had been brought into the community just to power this mill. The only other electrical devices at the Ark were the community's one telephone, some items that ran on batteries, and a record player owned by one of the elder Companions.

Also on the ground floor of the building was a complex of cold storage rooms; a chapel; a pottery workshop; and two spinning and weaving workshops. The women of the Ark spun wool from purchased fleeces, then wove it into cloth as weft, using mill yarn for warp. In this way, they produced a portion of the clothing used at the Ark, plus garments for sale. (Other clothes worn at the Ark were donated by friends around the country.)

Following the tour, Jane found some heavier, warmer clothes for me and sent me down to work with Jean-Claude and some visitors in the garden. The gardens covered two or three acres, and provided almost all the vegetables year-round for La Borie Noble. No chemicals were used.

In a separate operation, Jane had told me, a team of a few farmers from La Borie Noble raised grain on the Ark's 300 arable acres, using horses and, again, no chemicals. But most of this grain went to feed the horses and dairy cattle, so the community still had to purchase most of the grain used in its diet.

That afternoon, I cleared away branches and large twigs from one section of the garden, and also pulled a small plow that Jean-Claude guided. As in the morning, the bells tolled on each hour for prayers or silent reflection.

For supper, I joined some of the other single people in the kitchen, while other community members collected food there for family or small-group dinners in their apartments. At 8:00, the bell rang again, and the community gathered again in the Common Room.

Many of the Companions—who had first stopped in the downstairs chapel to recite their vows—were wearing brown, hooded cloaks trailing almost to the ground. We all stood along the edges of the candle-lit room. A wrought-iron candelabra had been placed in the center—an elegant piece, with candles on three arms stretching outward.

Shantidas was away from the Ark at this time, and was tonight replaced in leading the evening prayers by his chosen successor, Pierre Parodi.

O God of Truth,
Whom diverse men call by diverse names,
But who is one, unique, and the same...
Grant us understanding of your Law, Lord,
Wondering and compassionate reverence for all that
lives,

Love with no reverse of hate,
The strength and joy of peace.

As I came to learn, there were only a few prayers that were used on most occasions by the community. Some were written by Shantidas, while others were from traditional Christian sources—for instance, the Beatitudes from the Sermon on the Mount, and the Peace Prayer ascribed to Saint Francis ("Lord, make me an instrument of your peace.") But none of the prayers said anything that the follower of any major religion could not adhere to.

In fact, they had been chosen partly by that criterion. Though individually most of the Companions were strong Catholics, the Ark and its collective spiritual practices had no ties to any single religion; and adherents of any religion were welcome in the community. The Companions saw this as an important part of their nonviolent example, since religious intolerance so often creates conflict in the larger society.

Still, as one Companion later told me, this attitude did not come easy—even for the Companions. As she put it, "It is difficult to be enthusiastic for your own religion and respectful to others." Also, those professing no religion at all were less likely to be welcomed warmly as community members.

Following the prayers, Hirondelle led us in one of the songs of the Ark.

I had already been treated several times to this wonderful unaccompanied singing. It was no rough performance: Under the direction of Shantidas's wife, Chanterelle (who had died several years earlier), the Ark's singing had reached a state of fine art. The Companions had recorded a number of albums, which had twice won them an international award.

Most of the songs were original, usually on religious themes, and were full of majestic, vigorous harmonies. It was something like church music in the late Middle Ages, yet modern at the same time—a blend I was learning was typical of the Ark.

After the song, we greeted those on either side with a kiss on each cheek—the "kiss of peace." Small groups then remained to chat for awhile, before retiring for the evening. Exhausted as I was, I soon made my way to bed.

The next morning, though, I was up with the 5:00 tolling of the bell to join some others in the Common Room for an hour of yoga exercises and then meditation. At 7:00, the bell tolled again, and we walked out into the cold, where we were joined by others for morning prayers. Facing the rising sun, shining on us through the boughs of a large oak, we again were led in prayers and song. And morning prayers too ended with the kiss of peace.

The schedule I had followed over the preceding day was the same followed each weekday at the Ark. It was designed to balance the activities of the community residents and to provide a sense of rhythm, helping in finding an inner peace that would reflect in the outward.

The time for each activity was signalled by the tolling of the tower bell; but, as I soon realized, the Companions did not regard the bell as a master. Work was often started after the bell, or before; and, in fact, the bell-ringing itself was sometimes late—or missed completely.

The rhythm of the days was extended to a rhythm of weeks. This day, Friday, was a day not only of work, but also of silence and fasting until supper (though not everyone observed this rigidly). On the next day, Saturday, community work was stopped at noon; and, on Saturday night, young and some old gathered in the Common Room to folk dance far into the night.

On Sunday, many community members attended Mass in a nearby village, or in La Borie Noble's own chapel when a priest could arrange to visit; and the men took over cooking for the day.

Jane

These rhythms continued unbroken through most of my six weeks at the Ark, forming a warp through which I and the others wove the weft threads of our lives. As the days went by, I continued to work in the garden, at the woodpile, and in the storerooms when it rained or snowed.

In my remaining time I talked with Jane and others, studied French, and read the Ark's literature—mostly writings of Shantidas. I gradually came to more fully appreciate the principles underlying the Ark's way of life.

Chief among these was "bread labor," a principle that first gained wide notice through the writings of Leo Tolstoy, later to be adopted by Gandhi. This principle states that everyone who is able should assume a share of the physical work needed to provide life's basic needs—food, clothing, and so on. When some people avoid this necessary work (it goes on to say), their share of the work unfairly shifts onto the shoulders of others. Tolstoy and Gandhi saw in this the root of all oppression.

This idea does not by itself seem to explain all oppression in the modern West, or even in Gandhi's India. Still, the Companions seemed right about the importance of the *practice* of bread labor—everyone contributing work toward basic needs.

As the Companions pointed out, this practice almost automatically avoids much social and economic injustice. It practically insures that work is spread more fairly. It prevents division into classes of workers and non-workers. It also helps restrain material desires, which often grow past reasonable limits when someone else does the work to satisfy them.

For all these reasons, the Companions saw bread labor as the key to a nonviolent economy—an economy that abuses neither people nor nature.

While practicing bread labor, the Companions also aimed at self-sufficiency (though, as I had seen, they were still far from that goal). This was their way of removing support from our modern economy, which they saw as built on injustice—toward the poor, toward the Third World, and toward the earth. It was also their way of breaking their own dependence on this system, which they felt forces those within it into a sort of semi-slavery.

The Companions rejected machinery as being a product of human greed. Machinery was first developed, they said, so the rich could herd workers into factories and make bigger profits; it was also a way for Western society to produce more than it needed, or could even benefit from. Besides, if the Companions bought and used such machinery—along with the fuel or electricity needed to run it—they would tie themselves back into the system they were trying to quit.

From another standpoint, they pointed out that the use of simple tools benefits the health of the worker, both in body and mind. Also, their use discourages mass production, helping to avoid too heavy a burden on the resources of nature.

Crafts held a place of special importance at the Ark; in fact, the community's spirit was embodied in them. Objects were always to be made with an eye to beauty and elegance, never only to function. Each was to be carefully and lovingly decorated. Still, it was not the object that mattered most. The most important purpose of any work was to enrich the worker.

The Companions had chosen a hard life, but they didn't seem burdened by it. From what I could see, they attacked their work with a cheerfulness rarely seen in the "easier" jobs of modern society. In fact, they seemed to draw strength from it.

I was carefully watching my own reactions to the work I was doing. At first, I sometimes felt an inner resistance to it; but, almost at the same time, I found it was giving me a sense of peace. I couldn't say I enjoyed the work, but I still became absorbed in it. At the end of each work day, though I was very tired, I felt no great need to stop.

As time went on, I found the work was slowly changing my attitudes, "purifying" me. Grand plans and ambitions seemed to shrink to more reasonable size; labels I was bounding myself by seemed to fall away. I found myself more willing to live life in a small way, waiting for guidance. The rhythm of the days, the beauty of the hills, the movements of the hands—all these made me feel I was touching reality, maybe for the first time.

From my journal: *I know the arguments against those of us who would "return to nature." An answer to all of them lies wordless in my hands.*

Just as the Companions were trying to build a nonviolent economy, they had tried to build a nonviolent government as well.

The Companions saw modern government as built on violence, because its final authority rests on force, or the threat of it, from its military, police, and prisons. They didn't believe that force or violence against a person is ever justified, whether it is by individuals or by a government. When a government inflicts punishment on an offender, they said, the crime is not corrected, but doubled. In fact, they saw violence by government as more insidious than violence by individuals, because it hides behind a cloak of legitimacy.

For the Companions, a nonviolent government meant a government without compulsion—each person free to act as he or she saw fit. They felt no person or group should have power over any other, not even a majority over a minority. But at the same time, they realized, there must be ways for a community to act as a body, and ways to maintain order.

One of the Ark's solutions to this dilemma was to make decisions by consensus. No decisions were adopted without willing acceptance, if not full endorsement, by all concerned.

When the Companions had trouble reaching a consensus decision, they might step up their effort by fasting and keeping silence. When circumstances limited the time available for decision, the appointed leaders might be allowed to adopt a temporary solution, to be reviewed later.

The Companions met alone regularly to discuss their affairs, and at other times met together with other community residents. A *responsable*—coordinator—was appointed to look after each area of community work.

Each village also had a chief *responsable,* who helped carry out the community's decisions, handled small matters on a daily basis, and so on. The position carried no special privilege, and was rotated every other year. At the time, this position and those at higher levels were by custom reserved for men—though this has changed in the years since my visit.

Community discipline without coercion was the object of the Companions' system of "responsibility and coresponsibility."

"Responsibility" meant that each Companion was to watch over his or her own conduct. The standards to be upheld by such oversight included observance of the Ark's Rule (set of rules), and also of the Companions' seven vows. These vows were:

Work (including bread labor, service)
Obedience (primarily to the Rule and one's vows)
Responsibility (and coresponsibility)
Purification (of one's self)
Poverty (living simply)
Truthfulness (service of Truth)
Nonviolence (including defense of justice)

These standards were not seen as coercive, since the Companions had taken vows by their own free choice.

If a person did something considered wrong—like breaking a community rule, or failing to fulfill a commitment—he or she was expected to take on a suitable penance, whether or not the offense was known to others.

But, if the offender failed this duty, "coresponsibility"

came into play. Any other person observing the wrong was expected to approach the offender in private and point out the fault. Then, if the offender refused to acknowledge it, and the accuser remained convinced, *the accuser was to take on the penance.* The accuser might fast, or take on work the other had failed to do, or anything else suitable.

This was based on the idea that we each bear responsibility for the virtues and vices of every other. The hope, though, was that the offender, seeing someone else suffering in his or her place, would be led to recognize the fault and take on the penance. According to the Companions I talked to, this device was quite effective.

Both the Ark's government and its system of discipline came together at the head of the Order of the Ark, in the office of the Patriarch—Shantidas himself.

As Shantidas described it in his writings, the Patriarch's role was to enforce the Rule and basic principles of the community; and his word was law in such matters. There was no compulsion in this, he insisted, since the Companions had already freely vowed obedience to the Ark's Rule, to its "discipline," and to its guardians of these; and the Patriarch had no enforcement method more severe than "coresponsibility." The Patriarch himself was forbidden to give orders out of personal whim; and the position held no special privilege. In fact, part of the Patriarch's job was to work with manure.

Despite the constraints and lack of privilege, Shantidas seemed to hold more power than might be expected of one person in a "nonviolent government." But I learned from my talks with the Companions that Shantidas's written description of his job didn't reflect current practice.

The Community of the Ark

In the early years of the Ark, I was told, Shantidas did exercise a great deal of power. One reason given to me was that he had been almost the only one who understood what he was talking about; another was that the community had been unable to agree on anything. A firm hand, I was told, had been needed to keep the community running and on course.

But gradually the community had become more stable and united, with a "backbone" of about twenty older members to help guide it. As this happened, the Patriarch's authority gradually shifted to the Companions as a whole.

Now the Patriarchy was mostly an honorary position, and Shantidas had no more say than anyone else in the community.

This, I was told, had been hard for Shantidas himself to learn. A few years earlier, he had decided to send out many Companions, alone and in couples, to start new communities. But the Companions had told him they weren't prepared for that, and had simply refused to go.

Shantidas's successor, Pierre Parodi—chosen by Shantidas with the approval of the Companions—told me he saw his coming role mainly as that of a spiritual adviser.

It was a week after I had come to the Ark when Yvette Naal, one of the Companions, returned from a countrywide tour.

I had spent time with Yvette a year and a half earlier, when a tour brought her through San Francisco. She was in her mid-40s, though she looked ten years younger; a small woman, yet tough. I had been impressed by her strength and by what she had told me about the Ark; and that was why, in the course of a journey to visit "successors of Gandhi," I had made a point to stop here.

Yvette, a former travel agent, had been connected to the Ark since 1963 and had been a Companion since 1967. In recent years, she had joined Shantidas in the work of touring through Europe and North and South America, to speak about the Ark and to lead workshops.

These tours were one of the Ark's major forms of outreach, and Shantidas had been going on them almost since the community's founding. Now both Shantidas and Yvette spent most of their time away from the community. As one Companion told me, this was not a great sacrifice for Shantidas. He had founded the Ark because he believed in such community life; but, being himself a loner and habitual pilgrim, such life had never really suited him.

Out of these tours had grown a network of about fifty groups called "Friends of the Ark." The "Friends" studied Shantidas's writings, supported each other in trying to practice the Ark's principles, and took part in nonviolent actions. The Ark also recognized "Allies," who pledged themselves to follow the Ark's principles, but who weren't able to join one of the communities.

Though Yvette's correspondence was nearly full-time work, she managed to find time to walk with me to some parts of the Ark I had not yet seen.

One time we visited La Flayssière, the youngest of the Ark's villages, about a half hour's walk from La Borie Noble. The roughly twenty people who lived there were still busy restoring and remodelling the old buildings; some crumbled walls could still be seen. But La Flayssière already had its own garden, spinning and weaving workshop, and carpentry workshop. There was a youthful, adventurous spirit there, which made La Borie Noble seem established and almost sedate.

Another day, Yvette and I took the opposite path, up to Nogaret, the second village built by the Companions, where about thirty-five people now lived. Though not as youthful as La Flayssière, it too felt younger than La Borie Noble, and more intimate. Nogaret had plans to build elaborate workshops for the work and teaching of three of its Companions, master artisans in the traditional handcrafts of joinery (a branch of woodworking), blacksmithy, and stone-cutting.

The path through Nogaret led further, up past some ruined buildings that might one day be kernels for still more village communities. Finally we came to a high place, from where we could see both Nogaret and La Borie Noble far below, and mountains and valleys for many miles in every direction. In the distance, Yvette pointed out to me the Larzac plateau, a long table-land, where the Companions had been aiding a farmers' struggle against expansion of a military base.

On our walks and at other times, Yvette and I talked about aspects of the Ark—for instance, why the community was still far from self-sufficiency. There seemed many reasons. Poor, rocky soil and a short growing season kept the community's grain yields low. The Companions had had to build up their skills and most of the community's facilities almost from scratch. And many of the Companions were aging, and could no longer carry a full workload. Besides, much of the Companions' time was taken up by visitors—especially in summer, when the Ark could seem more like a training center than a community. Yet this form of outreach was considered by the Companions as too important to curtail.

There were other reasons, too. With my special interest in textile crafts, it seemed to me the Ark's women had yet to combine their eye for beauty with a practical rate of production.

I also suggested to Yvette that the Ark could come closer to self-sufficiency by giving up dairy products and eating the grain now fed to the cows. (It would also have brought them closer to their ideal of nonviolence. The Ark's male calves were sold to outsiders, presumably to be slaughtered for meat, as is normally done with these otherwise "useless" offshoots of dairying.) But Yvette—herself preferring a simple diet of raw fruits and vegetables—told me that most of the people there already considered it a great enough sacrifice to have given up meat.

"Actually, there are many ways we could live more simply," she said, to my surprise. "We don't need such fine buildings, and so much furniture. We could live more like the American Indians, in simple dwellings. That would be best."

Another of our topics was the roles of men and women at the Ark. I was concerned about the division of labor—women mostly cooking, cleaning, spinning, and weaving. Yvette tried to reassure me by telling me there were no restrictions written into the community's rules, and by pointing out occasional crossovers in work roles. But more important, she told me, "Men and women are not the same. They are equal to each other, but they're complements. We respect that difference."

I could accept that possibility to a point. But it still seemed that the Ark's sex role divisions outreached any natural differences.

Still, I could never have labelled the Ark's women oppressed. They had more presence and stronger characters than most women I had met elsewhere; and it was obvious they drew great joy from the life they had chosen. I also had to keep in mind that the community was still being guided by some of its earliest members (both men and women); and that, over time, the Ark would no doubt absorb more of the changes of the larger society.

From Yvette too I heard the story of the departure of the Ark's children. Around the late 1960s and early 1970s, a movement of charismatic Christianity swept over western Europe, and came as well to the Ark. Many of the Ark's young people were caught up in it, including the roughly fifteen young adults raised in the community.

The charismatic faith had an important difference from the spiritual beliefs of the Ark: It saw only Christianity as valid among religions. A few years before my visit, the issue had come to a head, when the young people called on all the Companions to declare the Ark a charismatic community. The other Companions refused—so the young people raised at the Ark all left. All except three now lived in charismatic communities.

I was shocked and puzzled at such behavior by those raised in a community holding religious tolerance as a basic principle. But later I realized that those who left may have acted on an even more basic tenet of the Ark: that everyone in the community should live by the same Truth. Even religious tolerance can be a dogma.

Another of my visits around the Ark was guided by Jane, when we went for a day of work at "the Mill." This was an abandoned sawmill the community was restoring in order to produce its own construction lumber from the Ark's forests. The work was being handled mainly by two couples, who were living there year-round.

One of those working there, an engineer named Michel, showed me a turbine left in place by the earlier owners. The stream that had once powered this turbine would be redirected to once again flow under the mill; the turbine would then directly power some machines, and turn a generator to produce 24-volt direct current to power others (including the Ark's flour mill).

After a morning of work in the garden, Jane and I gathered for lunch with the two couples and the baby of one of them. Michel was intrigued at hearing I was a Quaker, and asked me how Quakerism compared with what I found at the Ark. I told him there were many points in common: the striving after nonviolence and simplicity; a seeking to know and do the will of God; and also the use of consensus in governance.

One difference was that our ideal of material simplicity had traditionally entailed avoiding decoration, and letting the clean lines of a functional form speak for themselves; while, at the Ark, no object was considered complete without decoration. Also, we strictly avoided prescribed religious forms, such as ceremonies and set prayers.

Still another difference was that Quakers had no authoritative leader, other than what we jointly perceived as the inward voice of God; while the Ark had its officially-designated "Patriarch"—Shantidas. Michel and the others assured me that Shantidas had no more power in the affairs of the community than anyone else. Still, I insisted, Quakers would never officially set up even an advisory head.

In my turn, I wanted to know more about the work at the Mill. I asked Michel whether the use of heavy machinery and electricity didn't go directly against the Ark's principles.

"Some of the Companions opposed the Mill," Michel told me. "But the community finally decided it was better to produce lumber by machine than to buy it from outside." I could see that Michel himself had thought deeply on the issue and, while not seeing this solution as ideal, was satisfied it was the best at hand.

This visit to the Mill gave me much to think about. I agreed with the Companions on the benefits of hand labor and that it was a mistake to try to do away with it. But it seemed there was also a need to develop technology to make that labor more efficient. One of the main reasons the Ark was still far from its goal of self-sufficiency was that it simply did not have time to produce all it needed. A more efficient technology could have helped.

Gandhi's own view of machinery, I knew, had not been as extreme as the Companions claimed. He had approved machinery if it assisted skilled labor rather than replaced it; and even electricity, if its production could be decentralized. In fact, in the course of encouraging production of cloth in the villages, Gandhi had almost single-handedly developed the concept of appropriate or inter-mediate technology—though the terms came much later. (E. F. Schumacher was heavily influenced by Gandhi, calling him "the most important economic teacher today.")

Somehow a proper balance had to be struck between hand labor and more advanced technology. But it was a complex question; and, as far as I could see, there were no rigid guidelines.

These thoughts sparked others about the work I was doing at the Ark. After the first good effects, I had found myself growing restless and dissatisfied.

I now realized that hand labor must meet certain conditions to be fulfilling: It must claim the worker's full attention. It must be in step with the worker's abilities. Mental and physical effort had to be balanced, in a way suited to the individual. The worker had to feel that the work was useful, and that his or her effort was being used efficiently. The more I thought about it, the longer the list grew.

Some of these conditions were not being met for me at the Ark—so I had never struck the proper "rhythm." I felt, for instance, that I would have been much more satisfied doing some skilled craftwork, such as woodworking.

But I also knew I had not prepared myself by building such skills. In fact, I had avoided hand labor most of my life. So it was fitting that I should begin at the beginning, and work my way gradually towards jobs I would find more fulfilling.

One day, at one of La Borie Noble's community meetings, an announcement was made about a demonstration coming up in the nearby town of Millau. It was being organized by the farmers on the Larzac plateau in support of their campaign against the army base expansion. The Ark had been asked to send some people to help as monitors, and others from the Ark would be able to go along. I asked to go.

I had been reading some of Shantidas's writings on nonviolent action in the pursuit of peace and justice. I had learned that, for Shantidas as for Gandhi, the stated goal of such action was not to coerce the opponent into meeting demands. Rather it was to persuade him or her to willingly give up the behavior that was afflicting others.

To bring this about, Shantidas said, the nonviolent activist induces the opponent to multiply his or her misdeeds, to make their nature apparent. At the same time, the activist refuses to fight back, and in that way denies the opponent any opportunity for self-justification. Sooner or later, such action would awaken the opponent's conscience and bring about a change of heart.

Such action was undertaken not only for the sake of the victims; it was as well a duty to the opponent, who was suffering spiritually from these misdeeds.

For Shantidas, Gandhian nonviolent action was simply an extension of the teachings of Jesus. He pointed out

sayings of Jesus showing awareness of the power of nonviolent action: "If someone slaps you on the right cheek,
turn and offer your left." "Love your enemies and pray for
those who persecute you." According to Shantidas, it took
Gandhi to show the Christian world the force generated
when those words were taken seriously.

Shantidas had long been one of the foremost proponents
of Gandhian nonviolence in France and among Catholics
worldwide. (Pope John XXIII acknowledged Shantidas's
influence on his progressive encyclical, "Pacem in Terris.")
The Ark itself had carried out or helped lead a number of
nonviolent campaigns, all of them rigorous models of
Gandhian nonviolent action.

Most of these had been directed against French mili-
tarism and had taken place during the French-Algerian
War—the Algerians' fight for independence from France,
which lasted from 1954 to 1962.

The first of the Ark's campaigns took place in the
spring of 1957, when widespread practices of torture by
both French and Algerians were just beginning to come to
light. Shantidas, Pierre Parodi, and another Companion
undertook a 20-day public fast—taking water only—to try
to draw attention to the atrocities and to appeal to both
sides for their end. The fast drew much support from
among French religious circles and also appeared to be well
received by Muslim religious leaders in Algeria.

Shortly after, the Ark launched a nationwide organization called Nonviolent Civic Action. In 1958, this
organization ran a camp for training in nonviolent action,
which climaxed with an invasion of a nuclear research
center where France's nuclear bomb was being developed.

This was the beginning of the anti-nuclear movement in France, and the first-ever "occupation" of a nuclear power facility. (Companions are still active in the anti-nuclear movement.)

Meanwhile, the French government had begun keeping "suspect" Algerians in special internment camps, without trial or even formal charges. Nonviolent Civic Action waged a campaign against these camps, in 1959 and 1960. Thirty activists persistently tried to be arrested and assigned to the camps, declaring they were innocent citizens of France just like the Algerians, and so had as much right to be interned.

The government arrested the activists after almost every action, but wisely refused to imprison them. Still, the activists generated a great deal of publicity and support before giving up hope of entering the camps.

Later in 1960, Nonviolent Civic Action began a campaign to support the right of conscientious objectors to exemption from fighting—a right not legally recognized in France at the time.

The group issued a nationwide appeal to all draft-age men, and soldiers as well, who were opposed to war for reasons of conscience. It called on them to inform the civil authorities or their commanding officers that they could not take part in military service and to ask to perform civil service instead. They were then to leave right away for special service camps set up by Nonviolent Civic Action for work among the poor (usually Algerians); but they were to leave word with the authorities where they could be found.

If the police came for a young man, the leaders of the

work camp would promise to deliver him the next day at a certain time and location—normally, a public place at a busy hour. When the police arrived, they would find all the camp volunteers chained together, each claiming to be the one the police sought. Since the volunteers would be carrying no identification, the police would not be able to tell who was the right one—so they would have to arrest all of them.

Partly due to this campaign, the French government at the end of the war legalized conscientious objection.

Nonviolent Civic Action was dissolved after the war, purportedly to encourage local groups to take more initiative. But Friends of the Ark, singly or as groups, still took part in campaigns on a wide range of issues. In this way, the Ark was still indirectly linked to most of the nonviolent action movements in France. And the Ark itself had played an important role in inspiring and helping organize the struggle of the Larzac farmers, a struggle that had gained international attention.

The farmers had been trying since 1970 to stop the French army from taking over about a hundred family farms for the expansion of its base. They had publicized their cause with a number of creative nonviolent action techniques, including a tractor procession to Paris and, another time, trucking sheep to Paris to graze under the Eiffel Tower. (Their sign read, "Must the Larzac sheep come to Paris to find pasture?")

Groups and individuals all over France supported their cause; in fact, one demonstration had brought 100,000 people to the plateau. In almost a decade, the army had managed to obtain only a tenth of the land it needed.

The Larzac campaign—and through it, the Ark—had had more far-reaching influence as well. Larzac actions were part models for a later campaign to block building of a lead works at Marckolsheim in French Alsace with a non-violent occupation of the building site. Marckolsheim was in turn a model for a massive action against construction of a nuclear power plant at Wyhl, West Germany. And the Wyhl action directly inspired the first United States anti-nuclear "occupation," at Seabrook, New Hampshire— which initiated the country's entire direct action movement against nuclear power.

Early on the morning of the Larzac demonstration, about eight of us climbed into a van and rode about an hour to the town of Millau, on the other side of the Larzac plateau. (Neither the Ark nor individual Companions owned cars or trucks, but they sometimes used those of visitors and other community residents.)

It was bitter cold when we arrived at a small square at the edge of town. Gradually, other demonstrators gathered, many of them with banners proclaiming slogans and organization names. The farmers' supporters covered a wide spectrum, including regional separatists, Communists, and officials of Millau, plus many young people without apparent connection to any group.

The people I had come with from the Ark were given armbands, and assigned to helping direct the crowd. It was strange to see them, with their elegant, anachronistic dress and air of self-possession, moving within such a motley crowd. The people here seemed little different from those I had seen in demonstrations in the United States: Few could have had much understanding of nonviolent principles of the depth of the Companions'. Still, I overheard my friends being talked about with apparent respect.

After several hours of waiting, our procession finally started off through the wide, tree-lined avenues of Millau, led by a few tractors driven by Larzac farmers. From what I could tell, the stores we passed were all shut down, as part of a general strike called for that day in support of the farmers. Finally we reached the town's central square, where one to two thousand people stood listening to speeches for about an hour.

At the end, a speaker invited the crowd to meet on the Larzac that afternoon, to help plant a field owned and held by the army.

We from the Ark decided to stay for the afternoon action, and in the meantime drove up onto the Larzac to share lunch with one of the Ark's branch communities, Les Truels. Les Truels had been founded a few years before, on a farm that had been bought by the army for its base expansion and was being occupied by soldiers.

Two families from the Ark had first moved onto the farm by occupying some ruined animal shelters. They talked to the soldiers and baked bread for them and finally convinced the soldiers that they from the Ark should be allowed to stay. When the soldiers' superiors learned what had happened, they replaced this group of soldiers with another; but the same thing happened. Finally, the French Foreign Legion was called in.

But even the Foreign Legion proved no match for the friendliness of the people from the Ark. When the Legionnaires too succumbed, they were pulled out, and the farm left unguarded. The people from the Ark then moved into the main buildings and began restoring them, with help from people on the Larzac and other supporters.

After lunch, we went to help with the planting. About two hundred people, mostly in city clothes, were already there, clearing rocks from the ground and loading them onto trucks and wheeled platforms pulled by tractor. From the spirit there, it could have been a party.

A few hundred yards away, in clear sight, was a farmhouse flying a French flag. I was told soldiers were being quartered there.

After about an hour of rock-clearing, we moved off the field, and a brigade of Larzac tractors moved on and began turning the earth.

It wouldn't take long. After that, they would sow wheat; and the harvest would later go to hunger-stricken Third World countries.

As Shantidas had said, "How can the army touch us when we act in such a way?"

Palm Sunday.

The bell in the tower tolls, first weakly, but quickly building up strength to a full-bodied tone—then stops abruptly.

When I reach the courtyard of the main building, there are already people there, talking in small groups—people from La Borie Noble, from the Ark's other villages, and guests from the local area; others are still on their way on the paths from La Flayssière and Nogaret.

The people of the Ark wear their festival clothes, handmade all from white wool: the men with their heavy sweaters and pants, the women with their long dresses, and many of both with hooded cloaks down to their feet. The children rush around among the adults, then after awhile pass out boughs for the adults to hold. The sun shines brightly, though the air hanging between the tree-covered mountain slopes is still icy-cold.

Now all gather in a circle, each one holding a bough. Soon the singing begins: a hundred voices raised in stately, full harmonies.

Hallelujah!
Glory to God in the highest heaven,
And peace on earth to men of good will.

In the music, in the entire scene, the ancient and the modern seem to blend, giving a sense of timelessness. It is as if this could take place anywhere, in any time—while it is surprising to find it at all.

The mountains, the Companions, the music—it overwhelms me. *How can I ever describe this to people back home? How can they know the spirit of the Ark, without being here, without hearing this...*

The singing goes on and on, until it is time to enter the chapel for the morning's Mass.

Such was the beginning of the celebration of Easter at the Ark.

Few elements of community life were more important to the Companions than their festivals. These were the opportunities for the community to celebrate its unity and, by celebrating it, to strengthen it. And festivals provided the rhythms of season and year within which the rhythms of days and weeks could unfold.

Any reasonable excuse for having a festival was seized upon, so there were few months that passed without at least one. But Easter was among the most important. Preparations had been underway for weeks; and now friends of the Ark began arriving from all over France.

Shantidas arrived the day after Palm Sunday. He was just as imposing as he appeared in pictures. His great slender height, long flowing beard, aristocratic forehead— all these did in fact give him the air of a Patriarch. He was fascinating to watch in action, besides. The dramatic rise and fall of his voice was accented by contortions of his flexible face and by flowing waves of his arms that were followed along by the rest of his body. Children and adults gathered around him, vying for his liberal affections. Once a lion, now, at 78, he seemed like a kindly grandfather.

The Easter celebration resumed on Thursday with a ceremony called "the washing of the feet," and an all-night vigil in shifts in the chapel at La Borie Noble. The next day, a passion play by Shantidas was performed in a hall at La Flayssière, with the entire audience singing the songs of the play.

Easter Mass was held late Saturday night in the candle-lit chapel, crowded with people from the Ark in festival dress and with friends—all singing songs as the Mass progressed, and then afterwards until after midnight. This was followed, in the Common Room, by a holiday buffet and a full night of folk dancing. On Easter day itself, there were other special meals, another Mass, more folk dancing.

Festivals at the Ark could be exhausting. Monday, the next day, had been declared a day of rest. Still, I managed to rouse myself from bed that morning for an appointment with Shantidas.

I met him in his apartment, where I found him behind his desk, writing in longhand. As we talked, I noted that the sharp edge I had found in his writings seemed to have softened; but no expressiveness was lacking. He waved his arms as he spoke, hurling elegant phrases across the room. I thought I recognized the defense of one truly shy, who avoids close contact by hiding behind a dazzling manner.

I asked him about his views on machinery as compared to Gandhi's.

"Gandhi changed his views on machinery because of

pressure from his opponents," he told me. Even simple human-powered mechanisms like the bicycle were too complicated, he said, if they had to be *made* by complicated machines.

Referring to the work at the Mill, he said, "This is our weakness. *Of course,* we could cut the planks by hand. I saw that done myself, in my childhood. But this is a compromise, because we are not strong enough." As he spoke, he motioned toward pictures of machinery in a magazine on his desk, held up the fountain pen he himself had been using when I entered.

"Machinery is a worm with a hook."

I asked what were the greatest successes and failures of the Ark.

"Our greatest success is to have survived at all. Our greatest failure—we have developed much more slowly than I at first expected."

Did he feel the Ark could survive a major world crisis, as he had originally hoped?

"It may not be possible. How could we survive a nuclear holocaust? But at least we will remain as an idea and example to guide the survivors."

Our interview came the day before Shantidas was due to leave with Yvette for a tour in the United States and Canada. I was sorry I hadn't more time to get to know this person whom, from his writings, I had come so much to admire. Yet in a sense I *had* come to know him. I could see that the Ark was in many ways an extension of his personality, a reflection of him. Though he no longer held special power, the community was still founded on and guided by his thoughts, his sentiments, his vision.

I knew of few visions so worthwhile to follow. I had found at the Ark—as I had hoped to—a way of life that seemed sane; that approached nonviolence toward neighbor and nature; that built individuals strong in body, mind, and soul. And, joined to that way of life, I had found a profound spirit of peace and joy, a spirit that had touched me deeply.

Perhaps too I had found a direction. But whether or not this path proved mine, I knew that the Ark would ever hold a place within me.

That evening, for the first time, the weather was warm enough to hold evening prayers outside. A bonfire was built in the main building's courtyard. We stood in a circle, holding hands, as Shantidas himself led us in reciting his Prayer of the Fire.

We are all strangers and pilgrims. Let us light a fire at
the crossroads, to call on the name of the Lord.
Let us close the circle and make a temple in the wind.
Let us make of where we chance to be, a temple...
Blow on us, Lord! Blow our prayer into flame,
That our hearts of sticks and thorns and their fickle
spark of life may somehow serve your glory.

And after, the kiss of peace.

As timeless as the Ark seemed, it too must grow and change. And so it has, in the years since my visit, with another "village" at the mother community, another branch community (in a former abbey in southern France), and a doubling of the Companions, to more than 140 worldwide.

Perhaps the biggest change has been the passing of Shantidas, on January 5, 1981, while visiting a branch community in Spain. About five hundred people gathered at the Ark to attend his burial. By all reports, it was a marvelous festival.

Since then, both Jane and Yvette have informed me that women of the Ark have been coming into official positions of greater responsibility. Yvette writes, "After 35 years, there is the rising of a generation of mature women who are now capable to lead—and willingly... In his last years, Shantidas predicted it would happen." Also, Jane reports that men can now be found in the kitchen, helping with cooking and cleaning. "There has been some progress in nine years' time," she writes.

Shantidas's chosen successor, Pierre Parodi, has assumed his place as head of the Order. Softspoken, gentle in manner, and seemingly more of a family man than Shantidas, he has nonetheless undertaken the task of touring to spread the message of the Ark. According to Jane, he has not taken on Shantidas's title of "Patriarch" but is instead sometimes called *le Pèlerin,* the Pilgrim.

On Pierre's English-speaking tours, he is now more likely to be accompanied by Jane than by Yvette, as Yvette has devoted herself to helping seek peace in the Middle East. She has founded a small peace center in Jerusalem, affiliated with the Ark and with the International Fellowship of Reconciliation. In many small but important ways, she and her colleagues attempt to reconcile Jews and Arabs and to introduce nonviolent action as a substitute for violence in addressing grievances.

Other Companions too are involved in nonviolent struggles or peacemaking—in France, on such issues as uranium mining and racism toward immigrants. Internationally, Pierre has consulted on nonviolent action with anti-colonialists in New Caledonia; and the Ark has supplied personnel for a human rights team in Guatemala under the auspices of Peace Brigades International.

Some related news: The Larzac farmers have won their fight—at least for the moment. France's Socialist Party, after winning the national elections in the summer of 1981, announced it was cancelling the plans for expansion of the Larzac army base. The Larzac farmers responded to these developments by announcing a new goal: total removal of the army base from the Larzac Plateau.

Finally, the visitor to the Ark these years ago, the writer of this account, too, has changed. My drive to design and construct ideal social models is gone, replaced by an eagerness to play out creative possibilities in society at large. This has been part of an ongoing liberation from my own overbearing intellect, a loosening of bonds imposed by a domineering will to control.

Many motives can lead one to build, or live in, a

community. With the personal change described, my own have vanished. Yet I can never forget the sun on the hillside, the people of white raiment, and the song lifted high—to the Eternal.

Resources

Some books by Lanza del Vasto (Shantidas):

L'Arche Avait Pour Voilure Une Vigne (The Ark Had for Its Sails a Vine), Denoël, Paris, 1978. A collection of writings on the Community of the Ark. A publisher has not yet been found for the English translation.

Les Quatres Fléaux (The Four Scourges), Denoël, Paris, 1974. Philosophic critique of society. A publisher has not yet been found for the English translation.

Make Straight the Way of the Lord: An Anthology of the Philosophical Writings of Lanza del Vasto, Knopf, New York, 1974. Out of print.

Warriors of Peace: Writings on the Technique of Nonviolence, Knopf, New York, 1974. Out of print.

Return to the Source, Schocken, New York, 1972. Includes an account of Shantidas's stay with Gandhi.

By others:

Richard Deats, "'The Principle is the Unity of Life': A Conversation with Lanza del Vasto," *Fellowship* (date unknown). On the Ark and nonviolent actions.

Marjorie Hope and James Young, *The Struggle for Humanity: Agents of Nonviolent Change in a Violent World,* Orbis, Maryknoll, New York, 1977. Includes a chapter on the Ark.

Pierre Parodi, *The Use of Poor Means in Helping the Third World,* Greenleaf Books, Canton, Maine 04221, USA, 1970.

Oliver and Cris Popenoe, *Seeds of Tomorrow: New Age Communities That Work,* Harper and Row, San Francisco, 1984. Includes a chapter on the Ark.

Roger Rawlinson, *Larzac: A Victory for Nonviolence,* from Friends Bookstore, Friends House, Euston Road, London NW1 2BJ, England.

Mark Shepard, *Simple Sourdough,* Simple Productions, 12 East 15th Street, #3, Arcata, California 95521, USA, $2.00 postpaid. Recipe for wholewheat sourdough bread like baked at the Ark.

Addresses:

La Communauté de l'Arche
34.260 le Bousquet d'Orb
FRANCE

Letters to the Ark may be written in English. The community can supply books, records, and crafts it produces. Visitors are welcome for various periods and under various arrangements, but they must first write and wait for reply. Camps for English-speaking visitors are held each summer.

Greenleaf Books/Friends of the Ark
Canton, Maine 04221
USA

This group supplies books on the Ark (including books out of print), and maintains a network of people interested in forming a similar community in the United States.

Yvette Naal
Beit Noah
18 Ha Nevi'im
Musrara
97203 Jerusalem
ISRAEL

Yvette's peace center. Though the residents raise money through their own labor, the center and its work also depend on support from donations.

Index

About the Author

Mark Shepard's writings on social alternatives have appeared in over 30 publications in the United States, Canada, England, Norway, Germany, the Netherlands, Switzerland, Japan, and India. He is the author of *Gandhi Today,* on successors of Mahatma Gandhi in India and around the world. The American Library Association *Booklist* described *Gandhi Today* as "a masterpiece of committed reporting."